DODD, MEAD WONDERS BOOKS include WONDERS OF:

WONDERS OF WOODCHUCKS

Sigmund A. Lavine

Illustrated with photographs, drawings, and old prints

DODD, MEAD & COMPANY · *New York*

For Debbie—because I love her

ILLUSTRATIONS COURTESY OF: Annals of Carnegie Museum of Natural History (as photographed from book by Nicholas J. Krach), 28, 41, 42, 44, 48, 49, 58; Gouvernement du Quebec, Ministere du Loisir, de la Chasse et de la Peche, photos by Pierre Bernier, 9, 24, 26, and photo by Fred Klus, 59; Pauline Stoddard Howard, *The W. Chuck Family*, Copyright, 1920, by John Martin's House, Inc., 14, 21, 22, 55; Nicholas J. Krach, 16, 65; Sigmund A. Lavine Collection, 35; Jaro Malec, 67; Massachusetts Division of Fisheries and Wildlife, photos by Bill Byrne, 6, 36, 45; Museum of Science, Boston, Mass., 52; New York State Department of Environmental Conservation, photos by Nick Drahos, 27, 33; Jane O'Regan, 30, 57; Punxsutawney Groundhog Club, 17; Punxsutawney Groundhog Festival Committee, Punxsutawney Rotary Club, and Jefferson County Tourist Promotion Agency, 15, 19, 39; Shire Horse Farm, Cilshafe Uchaf, Fishguard, Pembrokeshire, England, 13; U.S. Fish and Wildlife Service, photo by Robert H. Hines, 54; U.S. Fish and Wildlife Service, photo by Dr. H. H. T. Jackson, 31; U.S. Fish and Wildlife Service, photos by Walter Lauffer, *frontispiece*, 69.

FRONTISPIECE: *Young woodchucks at entrance to den*

1   2   3   4   5   6   7   8   9   10

Library of Congress Cataloging in Publication Data

Lavine, Sigmund A.
   Wonders of woodchucks.

   Includes index.
   Summary: Describes the evolution, physical characteristics, and behavior of woodchucks and discusses their place in folklore, literature, and medical research.
   1. Marmots—Juvenile literature.   [1. Woodchuck]
I. Title.
QL737.R68L38   1984   599.32′32   84-1637
ISBN 0-396-08332-3

Contents

Emerging from a den hidden in tall vegetation, this wary chuck makes sure no enemies are nearby. Always alert, woodchucks are quick to spot potential danger.

1
Meet the Woodchuck

"A constant guest is never welcome."
—Heywood

Woodchucks have a long family history. It begins in North America during the Paleocene period, some seventy million years ago, when the chuck's remote ancestors first appeared. They were tree-dwelling, squirrel-like animals equipped with claws for grasping, tails for balancing, and chisel-like teeth adapted for gnawing.

As centuries gave way to eons, some of these creatures, unable to cope with climatic changes or to eat the new types of vegetation that spread across the Earth, vanished. Others adjusted to a variety of conditions and prospered. These survivors became the immediate progenitors of most of the animals that make up the order Rodentia to which the woodchuck and all other rodents belong.

Rodents, which vary greatly in form and habit, are gnawing mammals. They can be distinguished from all other animals by the structure and arrangement of the teeth. Rodents lack canines (tearing teeth) and have only one pair of incisors (cutting teeth) in both the upper and lower jaw. It is a characteristic of rodents that their incisors continue to grow, so enough gnawing must be done to keep them from becoming too long.

No one knows how many species of rodents exist. However, it is certain that rodents are not only the most numerous of animals but also the most successful. They thrive in every corner of the Earth from the Arctic to the tropics of the Southern Hemisphere, displaying an extraordinary ability to adapt to situations of all types.

Zoologists (students of animal life), faced with the tremendous task of classifying rodents, have divided them into three major groups: the porcupine-like rodents, the mouselike rodents, and the squirrel-like rodents. Among the tribes placed in the third category are the large, short-tailed, stubby-limbed, heavy-bodied, ground-dwelling squirrels known as marmots.

There are thirty-one species and subspecies of marmots. Both the yellow-bellied marmots that inhabit uplands in the western United States and the hoary marmots, residents of boulder-strewn areas above the timberline in the Rockies, have relatives in Asia and in Europe. But one North American marmot, *Marmota monax*—the so-called eastern woodchuck—has no Old World kin. All too familiar to amateur gardeners and commercial farmers alike, *monax* is found only from Labrador and Nova Scotia south to the northern parts of Georgia, Alabama, and northwestern Louisiana, west to eastern Kansas, and northwestward into Alaska.

None of the nine subspecies of *monax* is endowed with a great deal of intelligence. Nevertheless, the woodchuck is an excellent example of how rodents adapt and skillfully exploit new environments. Formerly, chucks were forest dwellers throughout much of North America, being particularly plentiful along the eastern seaboard. But in the 1770's, when colonists began to cut down trees in order to plant crops, woodchucks

Several subspecies of woodchucks range in various parts of Canada. This chuck (Marmota monax canadensis) *inhabits the greater part of the interior of Canada, and is also found in northern Wisconsin, southern Michigan, northern Minnesota, and northern Vermont.*

immediately moved into the newly created fields, where it was much easier to find the plants on which they fed. Incidentally, by taking advantage of the conversion of timbered areas into farmland, chucks became one of the very few animals that have benefited from man's felling of forests.

The woodchuck was first described under the name *monax* in 1747, when Mark Catesby published his account of the natural history of Carolina. Catesby did not invent *monax*—he had learned it from the Indians, who told him it meant "digger." Some years later, when animals were scientifically classified, *monax* was retained as the name of those marmots known as woodchucks.

It is far easier to trace the source of the woodchuck's scientific name than it is to determine the origin of its common name. There are those who claim that "woodchuck" is the English version of the Algonquin *wejack*. Others maintain that the name is derived from the Cree *otchek*. Still others hold that the term came from the Chippewa *otchig*. Actually, only one thing is certain—if either *otchek* or *otchig* was translated as woodchuck, an error was made. Both words are Indian names for the fisher, a large weasel hunted for its valuable silky fur.

Some students of etymology, the science that treats of the origin and history of words, are convinced that *monax*'s popular name is not a mistranslation of any Indian term. These individuals divide woodchuck into syllables and then define each of them. They explain that "wood" refers to the fact that *monax* formerly lived in forests, while "chuck" was once employed as a nickname for piglets—which, like woodchucks, have squat bodies and waddle.

Although there is considerable confusion about the source of the word woodchuck, there is none concerning "groundhog."

Woodchucks, like piglets, have squat bodies and waddle.

This name, given to *monax* in certain areas, is most descriptive for an animal that lives underground, spends much of its time rooting, and has a seemingly insatiable appetite.

Because woodchucks emit a shrill whistle when angry or frightened, they are sometimes called "whistle-pigs." But no chuck can whistle as well as its close relative, the hoary marmot. Under favorable conditions, the hoary marmot's whistle can be heard a mile away.

Although the habits of woodchucks living in various regions vary slightly due to environmental conditions, all chucks follow the same pattern of behavior. Therefore this book presents only the life history of *Marmota monax.* Its ways and wiles are typical of all the animals variously called woodchucks, groundhogs, and whistle-pigs.

2
Woodchuck Lore

"There are trifles, and old wives' tales."
—Marlowe

Only one animal has a special day on the calendar. Throughout the United States, the second day in February is known as Groundhog Day. Tradition holds that on this date woodchucks awake from their deep winter sleep and emerge from their dens. 'Tis said that if they see their shadows—a sign that winter will last for six more weeks—they immediately go back to sleep. On the other hand, if the chucks do not see their shadows, they remain outside their burrows, indicating an early spring.

German farmers who migrated to the New World in colonial times are responsible for the superstition that woodchucks interrupt their hibernating on February 2 for a weather check. Actually, these settlers imported European folklore. It is widely believed in the Old World that the badger comes out of the ground on Candlemas Day (February 2) to prophesy the duration of winter. All the migratory Germans did was to substitute the American groundhog for the badger.

No one knows for certain when the badger was first credited with the ability to forecast the weather. However, we do know

When German settlers brought European folklore to the New World, they substituted the groundhog for the badger. Pictured here are badgers in England.

that Candlemas Day was originally set aside by the Catholic Church some 1300 years ago to commemorate the purification of the Virgin Mary. How this feast day—at which candles are blessed—became linked with weather prognostication is a mystery. But the association was centuries old long before John Ray's collection of English proverbs published in the 1600's, included:

> If Candlemas Day be fair and bright
> Winter will have another flight,
> If on Candlemas it shower and rain,
> Winter is gone and not come again.

Truth to tell, there is some slight evidence to support the Candlemas tradition. If the sun is bright on February 2, making it possible for a chuck to see its shadow on the snow, the chances are that the weather is clear and cold and winter will continue.

Conversely, if it is rainy or cloudy and there is little snow on the ground, no shadow will be seen. Not only are such overcast days common during open winters but also they are frequently forerunners of an early spring.

Meteorologists laugh at the idea of a groundhog's shadow predicting future weather conditions. Experience has taught them that long-range forecasting is apt to be inaccurate, despite modern techniques. Meanwhile, zoologists have determined that chucks are not reliable weathermen. They reached this conclusion after studying weather reports for February 2 over a period of several decades. The research revealed that, more

"Let's go back to bed."

Charming illustration from an early 20th-century storybook shows the W. Chuck family and pet turtle looking out on Candlemas Day.

14

KING of the WEATHER PROPHETS
GROUNDHOG DAY FEBRUARY 2

Drawing shows the King of the Weather Prophets.

often than not, a shadowless Groundhog Day was followed by weeks of bitter winter weather.

Not only has the groundhog a poor record as a weather prophet but also field naturalists have learned that the majority of woodchucks are hibernating throughout February. Nevertheless, in Missouri, Groundhog Day has been officially established as February 2 by an act of the state legislature. Even though science has disproved the notion that the weather on Candlemas Day is an omen of a late or an early spring, winter-weary Americans eagerly await the news from Punxsutawney, Pennsylvania, each February 2. In this small Allegheny Mountain town, the Groundhog Club has kept watch over a wood-

Like their woodchuck relatives, prairie dogs dig burrows with vertical entrance shafts to which they flee at the slightest sign of danger. But while chucks lead solitary lives, prairie dogs are gregarious and live in "towns."

chuck's den every Candlemas Day since 1898. The newspaper photographers and television cameramen who flock to Punxsutawney are sure that they will see a chuck emerge from its den —it will be the pet of the Groundhog Club looking for an apple or some other treat.

Punxsutawney, the self-acclaimed "home of the traditional weather forecasting animal," is not the only community that engages in Groundhog Day activities. But Punxsutawney is the best known and gains additional publicity by ridiculing its rivals. For example, the Pennsylvanians accuse woodchuck watchers in Wisconsin of keeping a vigil over a prairie dog's den on Candlemas Day.

Long before Europeans settled in the New World, chucks were playing important roles in the legends of American Indi-

16

Punxsutawney Phil and James H. Means, president of the Punxsutawney Groundhog Club, photographed on a sunny day

ans. Although the Koska of British Columbia told of a huge man-eating groundhog, most tribes held the woodchuck to be an extremely clever animal and an ally of man. In fact, Cherokee tradition maintains that marriages between humans and woodchucks were commonplace "in olden times when animals used to talk and hold councils with the people."

A Mohawk tale explains why woodchucks dig dens. It begins in the days when the world was young and both humans and animals lived beneath the surface of the Earth. They might have remained there forever if Gamawagehha, the fire god, hadn't noticed a narrow crack in the Earth's crust. Wiggling through the opening, Gamawagehha emerged into a beautiful countryside bathed in warm light. When he returned to the Land of Darkness, Gamawagehha described what he had seen and suggested that animals and people migrate through the crack. Only the woodchuck refused to leave. From that time to this, so the story goes, chucks live contentedly deep in the ground.

According to the Penobscots and other tribes native to the northeastern United States, Glooscap, a culture hero, was accompanied by two comrades during his fabulous journeys. One was Mikumeau, a dwarf wood spirit with the power to increase his statue at will or to make himself so heavy that he would sink to his knees when standing on solid rock. While Glooscap relied on Mikumeau's skill as a bowman during their battles with supernatural monsters and evildoers, he never told the dwarf his plans. On the other hand, Glooscap had no secrets from his other companion—his grandmother, who followed him everywhere in the form of a woodchuck.

As is to be expected, the bewhiskered, buck-toothed woodchuck has not inspired artists to paint its picture. Nor has the

18

A lifesize bronze statue of the Punxsutawney Seer of Seers is located in the town plaza.

groundhog's squat body motivated many craftsmen to create representations of chucks out of stone, metal, or wood. Further, although the woodchuck has an extensive repertoire of squeals, grunts, and whistles, no well-known composer has been prompted to celebrate *monax* in song.

However, an unknown musician—most likely one lacking in formal training—who lived in the highlands of the South a century or so ago did write a comic ballad describing a wood-chuck hunt. Today, this rollicking tune with its spirited verses is considered a classic. Indeed, Alan Lomax, a leading authority on American folk music, maintains that "Groundhog" is "the best of all banjo pieces."

The woodchuck, although ignored by artists and practically overlooked by musicians, has not been neglected in literature. But while chucks scamper through the works of Henry Wadsworth Longfellow, Nathaniel Hawthorne, Oliver Wendell Holmes, and other well-known American authors, groundhogs have received scant attention from writers in the Old World. This is because European authors—and their readers—are unfamiliar with the chuck. Generally speaking, the only Old World publications in which woodchucks appear deal with customs, natural history, and travel.

Actually, even a well-educated Englishman could find Robert Frost's "A Drumlin Woodchuck" and Marion Edey's "The Jolly Woodchuck" most confusing. In England, woodchuck is the popular name by which the green woodpecker is known. However, once an Englishman understands that the poets are dealing with an animal, not a bird, he—like countless Americans—will enjoy Oliver Simon's "The Woodchuck Who Lives on Top of Mt. Ritter," Richard Eberhart's "The Groundhog," and David McCord's "A Woodchuck is a Groundhog."

Folk medicine has not endowed the woodchuck with any

The Alpine marmot is far more sociable than the woodchuck. It lives in colonies above the tree line throughout the Alps. A natural history published a century and a half ago credits monax's European relation with being very intelligent: ". . . the marmot is more capable of being tamed than any other wild animal. It will easily learn to perform feats with a stick, to dance, and in every thing to obey the voice of its master."

20

Fanciful children's book illustration shows how hard it is to wake a sleeping woodchuck.

Such as wet sponges and pulling off bed-clothes.

remarkable curative powers. However, North Carolinians claimed woodchuck soup was a specific remedy for whooping cough. New Englanders (who prescribed mare's milk for whooping cough) laughed at the idea of a chuck's being good for anything. Yet, strangely enough, Yankee farmers created a number of proverbs featuring the groundhog.

Many of these popular sayings are still in use in rural areas. In the hill country of Vermont and New Hampshire, an individual who is not overly bright "can't tell a woodchuck from a skunk," while a person in good health is said to be "sound as a woodchuck."

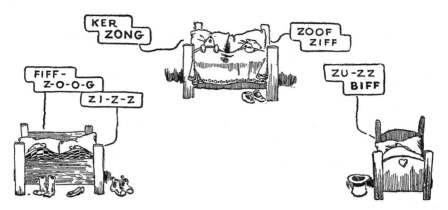

A sleeping chuck family

On the other hand, two woodchuck proverbs are known wherever *monax* is found. Both of these maxims stem from the animal's habits. Those who have no trouble sleeping brag that they "sleep like a woodchuck"—a reference to the groundhog's long hibernation. If someone states that he feels "like a woodchuck in clover," it implies that he is as happy and content as a chuck eating its favorite food.

One woodchuck reference is both complimentary and disparaging, depending upon how it is interpreted. Thus an attractive girl can either be annoyed or delighted upon hearing that a handsome young man has described her as being "cunning as a red fox or a gray woodchuck."

Generations of American youngsters have delighted in the tongue twister: "How much wood would a woodchuck chuck if a woodchuck could chuck wood?" However, not one person in a hundred can answer this familiar query. Can you?

If so, you know the correct response: "A woodchuck would chuck all the wood a woodchuck could chuck, if a woodchuck could chuck wood."

3
Physical Characteristics

"It is a familiar beast to man."
—Shakespeare

What color is a woodchuck?

This is not as simple a question as it appears. While both sexes are colored alike, immature chucks have paler fur than adults. Moreover, not only is there a slight seasonal difference in the shading of *monax's* fur—it looks brighter after the annual molt—but also there is considerable color variation among individuals.

Some woodchucks have orange-red fur. Others have pink hair. Still others are almost white or extremely dark. Albinism (the absence of pigment in the skin, hair, and eyes) and melanism (an overabundance of pigment in the hair and skin) occur in woodchucks. As a result, both snow-white chucks with pink eyes and chucks with deep black fur are occasionally seen.

While the yellowish, reddish, and pinkish cast of some woodchuck fur is quite attractive, *monax's* pelt is usually drab. Generally speaking, the upperparts of woodchucks are a grizzled brown, washed with a grayish or reddish cast, and frequently "frosted" with white. The underparts are pale brown or buff,

Albino woodchucks are quite rare. The white hair and skin on all parts of the body make it easy for hunters and predators to spot them. Albinos have very poor eyesight, which prevents them from seeing approaching enemies.

shading to white on the thinly haired belly. Face, head, legs, and tail range from dark brown to black. Nose, chin, and sides of face are a buffy white.

Woodchucks, like many furbearing animals, have two types of hair on their backs and sides: a short woolly underfur lies beneath the outer coat of long guard hairs. The undercoat is lacking on the belly, while the fur on both head and feet is quite short. In the spring when chucks enlarge old dens or excavate new ones, moving soil and stone with their heads, many of the diggers acquire bald spots.

Monax's fur is very coarse. Although John Burroughs, a pioneer American naturalist, wore a coat made from the skins of eighty chucks, no marmot fur has commercial value. Therefore, woodchucks have not attracted the attention of professional trappers. However, in earlier times, farm boys tanned chuck hides and used the leather for laces and whiplashes.

During the yearly molt, woodchucks resemble moth-eaten rugs. Chucks put on their new fur coats between May and October, older animals molting much earlier than immature ones. Starting at the tail, the faded hairs gradually fall out, each hair being replaced by a new one. This is an extremely slow process. It takes nearly a month for *monax* to complete molting.

General Appearance

As noted, woodchucks, like all marmots, actually are large ground-dwelling squirrels. They have heavy-set bodies supported by legs that are so short that the belly often scrapes along the ground. The short, bushy tail is flat, the broad head flattened, and the stubby nose blunt.

Both the ears and eyes are rounded. Because its ears, eyes, and nose are placed quite close to the crown of its flat head, *monax* has a built-in periscope. As a result, chucks can see, hear, or smell anything happening outside their burrows without exposing themselves to possible danger. All they have to do is to stick the top part of the head slightly above the rim of the burrow.

Size and Weight

The average woodchuck is between eighteen and twenty-seven inches long from the tip of the nose to the base of the six-inch tail, males being slightly longer than females. While most chucks weigh between six and ten pounds, a few individuals are unusually large. They may weigh as much as fifteen pounds.

Woodchuck weight, like coloration, varies seasonally. Chucks

Some thirty-one subspecies of woodchucks inhabit the United States and Canada. The monax *group is composed of nine subspecies. All of these animals, like the Canadian chuck pictured here, are generally brown with white-tipped hairs on the back. This gives them a grizzled-gray appearance.*

are lightest in spring when they awake from hibernation. Not only have they drawn on their stored fat during the long winter sleep but also many of the plants on which they feed have not yet sprouted. Conversely, *monax* is heaviest in the fall, after feeding all summer on succulent wild plants or cultivated crops. Incidentally, zoologists have learned that if a mature chuck and a young chuck are exactly the same length, the older animal will weigh more.

Legs and Feet

Although *monax*'s legs are short they are very powerful, being thick boned and muscular. Because the legs are so strong, chucks are able to use their paws as shovels and excavate tunnels and hollow out "apartments" that may be six feet or more beneath the surface.

As is to be expected, the feet of chucks are adapted for digging. Each front foot has four well-developed toes equipped with nonretractable claws as well as a knob-like thumb with a small flat nail. There are five clawed toes on the hind feet. When burrowing, *monax* loosens dirt with the forefeet and throws it backward with the hindfeet.

Few fossorial (digging) animals are more skillful than the woodchuck or as tireless. One scientist weighed the soil dug up by a small chuck in constructing its burrow and found that

Young chuck leaving its den concealed in high grass. The mound of dirt and stones piled in front of the burrow's entrance can be seen behind the chuck's hindquarters.

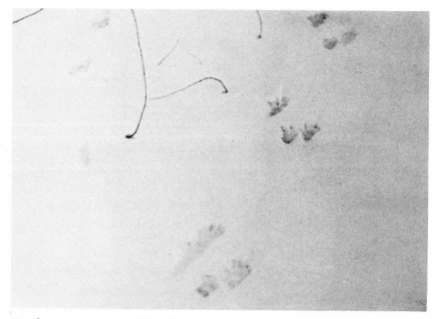

Tracks of running woodchuck in snow

it weighed seven hundred pounds. Another naturalist observed a seven-pound woodchuck move a fifteen-pound rock four feet. This is the equivalent of a 200-pound man carrying a 430-pound boulder the same distance.

In addition to using their small feet as tools for digging, chucks employ their paws to grasp objects. They can "select one particular blade of clover out of a clump and hold it daintily in both 'hands,' and eat it like a banana." The forefeet also serve chucks as scythes and pitchforks when collecting nest material. After tearing grass with their clawed paws, woodchucks stuff it into their mouths, carefully tuck in any loose ends, and carry the load to their burrows.

Like humans, the woodchuck is plantigrade, or flatfooted. However, *monax*'s tracks, which carry the imprint of the claws on all four feet, rarely show a clear impression of the full sole of a hind foot. Further, in the tracks made by a walking woodchuck, each hind foot usually overlaps the mark made by the front one.

Woodchuck tracks reveal whether the animal was running, trotting, or galloping. Tracks approximately four inches apart show that the chuck was walking. A separation of seven to nine inches between footprints indicates that *monax* was trotting, while a spread of eighteen to twenty inches tells that the woodchuck was galloping. Actually, a galloping chuck does not move very quickly—*monax's* top speed is from six to eight miles an hour.

Teeth

Zoologists derived the word Rodentia from the Latin *rodere* (to gnaw). In so doing, they called attention to the use rodents make of their sharp, constantly growing incisors. These cutting teeth are chisel like in shape and in action, as were the incisors of the rodents' remote ancestors.

Because the front surface of a rodent's incisors is composed of an extremely hard enamel and the rest of the tooth is considerably softer, the front edge lasts much longer than the back edge as the tooth wears. This gives the incisors their characteristic shape.

While the incisors of most large rodents are various shades of orange, those of *monax* are pure white. The cutting teeth of the woodchuck also differ from those of other rodents in another way—they do not grow while the animal hibernates. During the rest of the year, the teeth grow approximately one-sixteenth of an inch a week. Under normal conditions they do not become very long. The two incisors in each jaw are kept

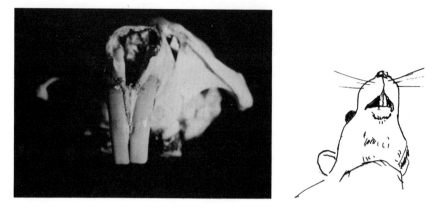

LEFT: *Photo of the incisors in the skull of a Norway rat;* RIGHT: *Drawing of a rodent shows incisors.*

short and sharp by grinding against one another as the animal feeds—the lower teeth putting a sharp edge on the uppers and vice versa.

Because of the construction of the jaw, which is connected to a series of complicated muscles, the incisors meet when the lower jaw is moved forward. Then, when a chuck switches from gnawing to chewing, the lower jaw moves backward and the incisors are positioned behind one another.

If injury or a malformity prevents the incisors from meeting, the upper pair usually curve back around and pierce the cheek-bone or the roof of the mouth. Similarly, the lower incisors may cut through the nose flesh and continue curving upward. Usually woodchucks that developed a malformed incisor are unable to eat or to gnaw vegetation and so die of starvation. Death also results if an incisor pierces the brain.

All told, *monax* has twenty-two teeth. Like all rodents, wood-chucks have a gap between their front teeth and their high-crowned cheek teeth. When the lower jaw moves forward, the cheek teeth do not meet and chucks, by drawing in the cheeks behind the gap, can shut off the back part of the mouth. This not only enables woodchucks to gnaw for long periods without swallowing but also prevents unnecessary wear on the cheek teeth. Meanwhile, the only time the upper and lower cheek teeth come in contact is when a chuck moves the lower jaw backward, stops gnawing, and begins to chew.

Monax not only uses its teeth to harvest and to grind vegetation but also employs them as a tool and weapon. When digging, chucks easily cut through roots four inches in diameter with their incisors. Their cutting teeth can also inflict serious wounds. However, chucks prefer to run for cover when they sense danger.

Here's a happy chuck! It has found a stand of juicy grasses and is stuffing its mouth as fast as possible.

The peace-loving chuck becomes a demon when aroused. Although it would rather run than fight, few animals are more courageous in the face of an attack. *Monax*'s bravery was noted by naturalist William Cram in 1902 when he wrote, "If cornered, he is ready to fight anything and anybody, and a Dog, lacking experience . . . is likely to get the worst of it."

Cram was right. However, dogs that are skilled hunters have little difficulty in killing chucks. Nor do the woodchuck's sharp incisors protect it from its worse enemy after man, the red fox.

Senses

Woodchucks have exceptionally keen senses of smell, sight, and hearing. As a result, chucks, which are timid creatures and easily alarmed, usually receive ample warning of potential dangers. If ears, eyes, or nose inform *monax* that a dog, human, or other predator is nearby, it immediately dives underground.

HEARING.   It is not easy for a man or a beast to sneak up on a chuck. *Monax* can hear the rustle of dry grass or the noise made by the breaking of a small twig more than two hundred feet away. Although, as noted, chucks are rather stupid, they do learn to associate danger with certain sounds, such as gunshots. W. J. Schoonmaker, a naturalist specializing in the study of woodchucks, reports that in areas where hunters drive along rural roads looking for woodchuck targets, the animals run to their dens at the sound of an approaching automobile.

Incidentally, human mothers have reason to envy woodchucks with young: no matter how much digging the babies do, they never get dirt in their ears. *Monax*'s rounded outer ears fold over the ear openings automatically when the dirt begins to fly.

SIGHT.   *Monax*'s eyesight is as sharp as its hearing is acute. Al-

This chuck has spotted a potential danger. Note the set of head and position of ears, eyes, and nose. All are in a line directed toward the source of the chuck's alarm.

though woodchucks are apt to suffer from blurred vision immediately after awakening from their winter sleep, this condition soon vanishes and *monax* has no difficulty seeing distant objects. One naturalist, observing chucks seven to eight hundred yards away through field glasses, gathered ample evidence that the animals saw him clearly. Confident that they were safe at that distance, the chucks did not run to their dens but continued feeding, keeping a sharp watch on the intruder. If these chucks had been hunted or otherwise molested by man, there is no doubt that they would have gone to earth immediately.

SMELL. As noted, woodchucks rely upon their keen noses as well as their ears and eyes to determine whether or not it is safe to leave their dens. Chucks also smell the dirt around the entrance to their burrows when they return, checking to see if any unwanted visitors came calling during their absence.

A woodchuck's nose is not employed solely as an "early warning system." Smell plays an important part in social contact between individuals. In the spring when chucks are seeking mates, the males go from den to den, sniffing the dirt piled up in front of each burrow. Their sensitive noses tell them whether a den is occupied, and if it is inhabited by a male or a female or a mated pair.

Voice

Woodchucks make a variety of sounds. The one most often heard by humans is the alarm call—a short, shrill whistle preceded by a low *phew*. The alarm call—which is often followed by a slowly fading warble that sounds like *tchuck, tchuck*—is very similar to the whistle some people create by placing two fingers between their teeth. Because the two whistles resemble one another, it was formerly believed that chucks actually pro-

Print by Audubon shows old and young woodchucks. Note the teeth, the feet, and the large chuck seated on its platform.

duced their alarm call by putting two of their clawed toes in the mouth!

The type of sound made by a chuck depends upon whether it is angry, curious, or frightened. For example, when annoyed, a woodchuck will emit a chattering bark, then gnash its teeth. If startled, *monax* combines chattering with a low-pitched whistle. Frightened woodchucks grind their teeth, snarl, and squeal. Females communicate with their babies—which have a pleading cry similar to that of human infants—by a series of barks and grunts.

Woodchucks that have adjusted to captivity express their contentment by purring. But no observer of woodchucks has ever heard one sing, as did a certain Dr. Albert Kellog who lived in Maryland in the 1800's. Dr. Kellog claimed that the woodchuck was "able to sing like a canary bird, but in a softer, sweeter note."

35

Caught offguard, the photographer did not get a clear picture of this chuck dashing to its den. At top speeds, woodchucks run about eight miles an hour.

4
Ways of the Chuck

"You must look where it is not, as well as where it is."
—Fuller

Woodchucks are creatures of habit. Thus if one is being chased and is cut off from the regular runway that leads from feeding ground to den, *monax* still will make an effort to reach his well-worn path, even though it would be faster to dash directly toward the den. Further, the chances are excellent that if a trap has been placed in the path, the chuck will enter it. Indeed, woodchucks are captured time after time in traps set in the very same spots.

Yet, despite its lack of intelligence, *monax* not only knows enough to stay alive but also to prosper. This seems to indicate that being a creature of habit must have advantages. Examining the behavior of chucks throughout the year, beginning with the winter months when woodchucks hibernate, will show if this is so.

WINTER

Bedtime

Animals native to the temperate zone meet the rigors of winter in various ways. Numerous species of birds migrate to warmer regions. Other creatures prepare for cold weather and a seasonal shortage of food by becoming sluggish, thereby lowering energy requirements. Still others fall into a fitful sleep, awakening now and then to prowl about. But *monax* is a true hibernator. During its long-lasting sleep, a slumbering chuck is so immobile that it seems to be lifeless.

Woodchucks instinctively begin to prepare for the next hibernation immediately after emerging from their dens the preceding spring. They spend a great deal of time eating and, as a result, accumulate considerable fat. As one naturalist notes, "Fat is absolutely the number one requisite for successful hibernation. In fact, without being thoroughly upholstered, the animal cannot survive the winter."

Woodchucks accumulate two types of fat. One is a thick blanket of white fat that not only acts as insulation against cold but also supplies the body with nutrients. As white fat is slowly consumed by body processes, it furnishes the cells with nourishment.

The second type—a brown fat—is identical to that found in many newborn mammals. Most lose this brown fat—which enables infants to warm quickly without shivering—when they mature, but woodchucks and other true hibernators retain their brown fat cells in adulthood.

Layers of the brown fat form a cape around a chuck's neck that reaches down the back between the shoulder blades. This cape insures that the central nervous system and the nerves that control the limbs are well buffered from the cold. A thick covering of brown fat also encases the kidneys, protecting them so they will not be damaged and will function perfectly.

Beside developing layers of fat, chucks also store up reserves of vitamins C and E during the summer. Research has revealed that these vitamins are of vital importance to hibernators. Vita-

Woodchucks accumulate fat before hibernating. Note the fold around this chuck's head and shoulders.

min C wards off infections, while vitamin E plays an important part in regulating the rate of body processes.

Some woodchucks native to northern regions where winter comes early and spring arrives late spend three-quarters of their lives asleep. However, generally speaking, chucks inhabiting the most northern reaches of *monax*'s range begin hibernating about the middle of September. Two or three weeks later, woodchucks native to New England start slumbering. Their kin in the southern states may not enter their dens and curl up for the long winter sleep until late October.

Incidentally, the resident woodchuck population of any region does not go into hibernation as a group. Weeks may pass before all are asleep. Sometimes chucks are seen after a snowstorm near dens in open fields. Because these individuals are in open country, it is safe to assume that they are immatures not fat enough to hibernate and thus are desperately seeking food. Another indication that these wakeful chucks are young is the fact that adult woodchucks usually dig their hibernating dens in spots sheltered by trees and shrubs. It well may be that the temperature in such protected areas is higher than in windswept fields or on the sides of hills. Then, too, frost may not be

Chucks have dug dens near shrubbery on this southern-facing slope for generations.

able to penetrate the leaves that are scattered like a thick rug over such burrows.

Chucks hibernate on previously arranged bedding in a sleeping chamber—a room dug at the end of a tunnel or excavated in one of its sides—that is always below the frost line. To keep out intruders, chucks scrape dirt off the back wall of the bedchamber and use it to make a tight "door." Although captive chucks do not seem to resent being forced to hibernate with bedfellows of both sexes, most wild chucks demand complete privacy when they sleep.

Nevertheless, while digging up dens during the winter, zoologists have discovered that two woodchucks do hibernate in the same den at times. In most instances, the two are youngsters of different sexes that will mature when they emerge in the spring. Observation has revealed that these individuals usually continue to live together and mate.

40

Deep Sleep

Once a chuck has sealed off its tomblike bedroom, it flops on the bedding it has collected, arches its back, and rolls into a ball. The ball is so compact that the shoulders and part of the head rest on the ground. The nose is tucked between the hind legs and paws, the front paws enclose the shoulders, and the forward-facing tail may cover the head. Occasionally chucks curl up and then lie on one side while hibernating, but most of them resemble balls of fur when asleep.

Monax does not go into deep sleep immediately. At first a chuck catnaps sporadically, the periods of sleep becoming longer and longer. Eventually, the animal is in a deep slumber. Now its breathing slows down. Awake, *monax* takes six breaths

This hibernating den is most unusual. The roof of the bedchamber is only a foot below the surface of the ground.

Rearing cages for woodchucks. The nest chamber and pipe "burrow" are covered with straw when in use.

a minute, while hibernating it takes but one. Meanwhile, the body temperature drops from a normal average of 96.8°F. to 37°F. While these changes are taking place, heart beats are reduced from 150 a minute to five or ten, and far less blood flows to those parts of the body behind the rib cage than when *monax* is awake.

Popular opinion holds that it is impossible to rouse a hibernating woodchuck. This is not true. The groundhog may not wake immediately if prodded or shaken, but it will stir. If the chuck does wake up, it will look curiously around, curl up, and go back to sleep.

In observing colonies of captive woodchucks, zoologists have discovered that their experimental animals do not sleep soundly all winter. Chucks raised at the University of Maryland awoke about every ten days and their temperatures rose to approximately 98°F., remaining there for the next twelve hours. During this period, the chucks were wide awake but went back into hiberation for another ten days or so when their temperatures dropped to 38-40°F. This cycle was repeated over and over throughout the winter.

While it is most likely that wild woodchucks awaken occasionally during hibernation, no naturalists have gathered data to confirm it. Nor have we any actual knowledge of how free-roaming chucks act when they awake from hibernation and get ready to leave their dens. However, zoologist George J. Johnson reports:

> Two types of awakening from hibernation have been described. . . .(a) A relatively rapid awakening accompanied by trembling and shaking of the head and shoulders, following a disturbing of the animal. . . .(b) A more gradual awakening, usually without trembling or shaking, after removal without disturbance to a warm room . . . this type of awakening is probably typical of that in nature.

Out of Bed

Because of the difference in weather conditions throughout *monax*'s range, woodchucks in some areas appear much earlier than in others. However, neither free-roaming chucks nor captive specimens emerge from their dens until the days grow warmer. There are exceptions to this general rule: individual chucks may dig their way out of their snow-clogged burrows long before any of their neighbors are awake.

When a woodchuck comes out of the ground in the spring for the first time, it bears little resemblance to the chubby creature of the previous fall. While hibernating, chucks live on the one-half to three-quarters of an inch of fat under the skin and in the body cavity and consume most of it. Indeed, during its four- to five-month fast, a woodchuck can loose between

43

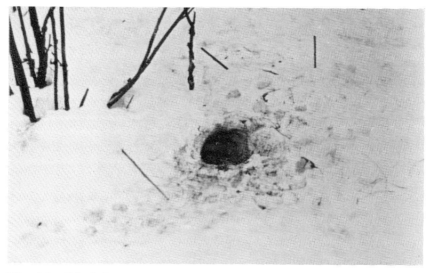

Woodchuck hole in snow

one-third and one-half of its autumn weight. Now, lean and hungry, *monax* is desperate for food.

But finding food is not an easy task—snow may cover the countryside, or the vegetation on which chucks feed may not have sprouted. Thus a chuck may continue to lose weight, but as soon as green plants are plentiful not only is the fat utilized during hibernation replaced but also chucks begin to get heavier.

Male chucks are usually the first to leave their dens. Although hungry, they spend more time looking for mates than for green grass on the south side of sheltered hillsides where the snow may have melted. The search for females is a danger-filled adventure. Not only do males have to be on guard against both winged and four-legged predators but also they must watch out for rivals determined to defend their territories. Despite these risks, male chucks intensify their attempts to find mates as spring days grow warmer.

Boy Meets Girl

While young males that are mating for the first time may wander aimlessly for days before encountering a female, older males waste no time. Familiar with the location of all the burrows in their neighborhood, they go directly to them. As indicated, their sense of smell informs them whether the occupant of a particular burrow is a male, female, or a mated pair.

If two males arrive at a female's den at the same time, they fight. When the rivals are evenly matched, the battle is bloody. First the combatants growl, grind their cheek teeth, and then rush at each other. Squealing with rage, they tumble about, inflicting gashes on flank and back with their sharp incisors. Grizzled veterans of these conflicts are easily recognized—parts of ears and tails have been bitten off and they are badly scarred.

The winner wins the right to enter the burrow. He goes in

When male woodchucks gnaw the outer bark of saplings in early spring, they are doing two things at once. Not only are they enjoying a delicious meal but also they are marking their territories.

This girl is standing on the site of a woodchuck den. Though she has long since grown up, chucks still build their nurseries on this sunny slope near a large rock, and can be "whistled-up" by passersby on an adjacent road. The clear space around the den gives a good view of the surrounding area.

with tail wagging. But the happy victor may not get a hero's welcome. A female chuck is unpredictable. She may accept a suitor or drive him away. A male chased out of a den may return to it a dozen times. Often his persistence is rewarded and he is permitted to stay. If "jilted," he is ejected violently.

While females mate but once each spring, some males are polygamous. However, most males remain with one female. The two live in her den until just before the young arrive.

Preparing the Nursery

Baby chucks are born from early April to mid-May after a gestation period of twenty-eight days. Pregnant females prepare for the arrival of young by evicting their mates. If one should lack the strength to drive a big and powerful male out of their den, she moves. If an abandoned den is available, she will take possession of it. If not, a new one is dug, preferably on an open hillside. Such a location is sunny, has good drainage, and provides food, while the lack of trees allows a clear view of the surrounding countryside.

Whether the den is old or new, a nursery is prepared—a small chamber in which a nest composed of soft vegetation and dried grass is placed. When gathering nest material, females, particularly young ones, are extremely nervous and collect plants as fast as possible, constantly looking in all directions for potential danger. Yet, even though woodchuck nurseries are prepared in haste, all of them look as if they were made by the same individual—their measurements are practically identical.

Woodchuck Babies

Female woodchucks produce litters containing from two to nine young, the average number being four. The dark-pink newborn are about four inches long and weigh between one and one-and-a-half ounces. Naked, blind, with forelegs more developed than the hindlegs, the infants are totally helpless. Their mother carries them about the den by taking hold of the wrinkled loose skin between the shoulders with her teeth.

When the youngsters are two weeks old, a soft, grizzled gray fur covers the head and body. This gives way to a most attractive golden-tinted coat. Meanwhile, the babies, having learned to crawl, are very active and constantly hungry. When nursing them, the mother either stands on all fours or sits up on her haunches.

By the time the litter is four weeks old, they are nibbling at the vegetation brought into the den by their mother but continue to nurse. As the days pass, their eyes open and the babies develop adult coloration. The young now scamper after their parent when she leaves the den, to play and to feed under her watchful eye.

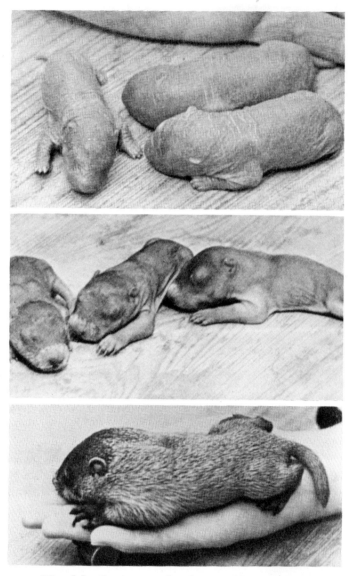

ABOVE, TOP: *Woodchuck pups twelve hours old;* MIDDLE: *Two-week-old chucks with grizzled snouts;* BOTTOM: *A "handful" at four weeks.*

OPPOSITE, TOP: *Playful five-week-old woodchuck pups;* MIDDLE: *Young woodchucks seven weeks old;* BOTTOM: *Woodchucks at eight weeks.*

Mother Knows Best

Woodchuck pups receive neither care nor instruction from their fathers. Males are not allowed to go near their offspring. Mothers take complete charge of the babies. Although loving and affectionate, females are strict parents. It is well that they are—their instruction may enable a pup (if it is extremely lucky) to live for five or six years, the average lifespan being between two and four years.

Always on guard against potential danger, mothers keep a watchful eye on their pups as they feed and play. If a pup ventures more than a few feet from the burrow's entrance, it is dragged back by the neck. From the first day pups go above ground, their mothers begin to teach them to stay close to the den so that they can dash into it with ease if threatened.

To insure that their offspring will know what to do in an emergency, the females conduct "drills." Pretending they have spotted a predator, mothers give false alarms, to which the pups respond by fleeing to the den. This exercise is repeated over and over. Pups that do not move quickly enough may be given a gentle nip. Thus it does not take long for chucklings to acquire the habit of going underground, where it is relatively safe from dogs, foxes, hawks, and other predators.

Between drills, mothers let the youngsters climb all over them, nuzzle, and touch noses. But even while caressing her babies, a mother is alert and, if she senses trouble, will roughly push the pups aside so that she can investigate whatever has attracted her attention. If there is no need to sound an alarm, the mother resumes playing with her brood. The love displayed by female chucks for their offspring and the great concern they show for their safety disproves the widely accepted belief that a female will push a pup or two out of a den in order to distract a predator and thus save her own life.

50

Chucks thrive in summer. During the warm months, there is an abundance of alfalfa, clover, various grasses, juicy bark, berries, wildflowers, and cultivated crops on which to feed. Ninety-nine per cent of *monax's* diet consists of plants; the remaining one per cent is made up of grasshoppers, June bugs, and other insects. Some chucks vary their menu by dining on the eggs and young of ground-nesting birds.

Chucks consume food equal to one-third of their weight everyday. This is equivalent to a 180-pound man eating sixty pounds of food in about twelve hours! Although chucklings do not gain weight as rapidly as adult woodchucks, they do grow heavier and heavier. Before long the brood chamber is too small to shelter them. Mother chucks prepare for this overcrowding either by digging a den or remodeling an abandoned one for each of the pups. But they continue to watch over their offspring—visits to them becoming more infrequent as the weeks pass—until fall, when the young chucks will establish territories of their own where they will set up housekeeping.

Easy Living

Woodchucks engage in two main activities during the summer. They eat and bask in the sun. Chucks of all ages delight in taking sunbaths on the tops of boulders, on stumps, stone walls, or the mound of soil in front of their dens. When basking, they lie in a prone position, legs extended and body flattened in order to get the most exposure. While being warmed by the sun's rays, *monax* often takes a short nap, in addition to sleeping from nine to ten hours in its den.

Although chucks enjoy the sun, they do not mind inclement weather. They go out to feed every day, even if it is raining heavily. Indeed, *monax* appears to like wet vegetation. Un-

Woodchucks feeding and sunbathing on rocks near den

doubtedly this is because it supplies fluid. Woodchucks do not drink water but get all they need from dew-covered plants and the juices of fruits. Whether eating dry or wet food, chucks either grasp it with one paw and carry it to the mouth while standing on three legs or squat on their hindlegs and use their forepaws like spoons.

Chucks rarely forage more than one hundred yards from their dens except when food is in short supply. But *monax* will climb trees in order to dine on ripe fruit thirty or forty feet above the ground. After gorging, a chuck will settle down between two branches and catnap before descending headfirst. Nor will chucks hesitate to take to the water in order to reach a favorite food, even if they have to dogpaddle a considerable distance.

52

Pests and Perils

Summer not only brings warmth and plenty of food to *monax* but also a swarm of pests. Fleas, mites, ticks, and various other tiny creatures, some merely annoying, others capable of causing death, parasitize woodchucks. This explains why chucks are often seen scratching with their hindlegs or brushing one fore-paw against the other to relieve the sting of a bite or to stop an itch.

As noted, woodchucks have to be on guard constantly against predators. This is particularly true in the summer when they spend a great deal of time above ground. Individuals living in meadows are apt to be preyed upon the most—when the grass is cut for hay they can be seen easily by men and dogs. Chucks in the open are also quickly spotted by foxes and the other predators that feed on them. In some parts of its range, *monax* has to be on the lookout for black bears or bobcats. Mink and weasels are their biggest worry in other areas. Also chucks are killed and eaten by large hawks and owls, coyotes, and wild-cats. Incidentally, occasionally a large rattlesnake will kill a chuck. Because of predator pressure, dogs, hunters, and the widespread use of traps and poison, only a small percentage of the chucks born each spring live for more than a year.

Not only do chucks have to be on guard against their enemies but also they have to protect themselves from members of their own species. While fights between adult chucks are rare outside the breeding season, youngsters that venture into established territories while seeking a home range of their own are sure to be attacked vigorously. The trespassers usually retreat as fast as possible, "knowing" that they are no match for the older animals. If the unwanted visitor is overtaken, a fight ensues. These battles, which are not as violent as those between rival

The chuck shown here is making sure there are no enemies close by before beginning to feed. Few animals are more alert—or more curious—than monax.

suitors, help keep a local population of woodchucks healthy and strong. By driving young chucks away from their birthplace, the adults prevent interbreeding—the mating of members of the same litter—which often produces young that are weak or deformed.

Autumn

By late August, the majority of woodchucks that have survived the perils of summer are best described as roly-poly. As the nights grow crisper and leaves of hardwood trees become tinged with brilliant colors, adult chucks become less active. They spend much of the day dozing in the sun in front of their summer dens.

A likely den spot

Young chucks have little time for sunbathing unless they had no difficulty in acquiring a territory and have prepared a den in which they can hibernate. By the time they are two years old they will, like most chucks, have two residences. One of these is a summer den situated at the edge of a field or on a gentle slope not too far from where the chuck forages. This den is occupied from late spring to early fall.

The second den is usually used only for hibernation although it may be lived in throughout the year. As noted, winter dens are always excavated in sheltered spots: the edge of a wood, under a rock pile, or beneath a stone wall. Chucks prefer to locate their winter dens where the ground slopes gently, but they will not choose any site unless there is good drainage. A much sought after winter "address" is among large roots protruding from the ground. Because of the roots, predators cannot enlarge the den's entrance to reach its occupant.

Chuck Cottages

It does not take a great deal of skill to excavate a winter den. There is rarely more than one entrance, which is connected to a tunnel leading to a sleeping chamber well below the frost line. The chamber is where the owner of the den hibernates.

However, constructing a summer den in which to live and perhaps mate and raise a family is a complicated piece of engineering. While all summer dens have the same characteristics, they differ in depth, number of entrances, and the length and diameter of the tunnel leading to the living quarters.

The type of soil determines how far below the surface the chambers are located as well as the length of the forked tunnel that leads to them. Dens are deeper and tunnels longer in sandy soil than in rocky soil. Irrespective of the character of the soil, chucks excavating winter dens first dig straight down from three to six feet and then begin to clear the den's main shaft. The average shaft is between fourteen and twenty feet long but some chucks dig extremely long tunnels. The longest ever recorded was forty-seven feet.

No matter how long or short it is, the main tunnel leads to a sleeping chamber and two or three other rooms. One of these is used as a toilet. Woodchucks are very clean animals and either regularly remove excrement from their toilet rooms or block the rooms up and dig others when they are needed.

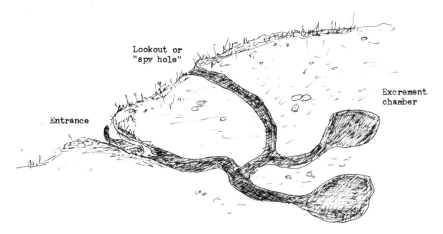

Lookout or "spy hole"

Entrance

Excrement chamber

Constructing a den is a feat of engineering.

Chucks also seal up chambers no longer in use that were reached by side galleries branching off the main tunnel.

All summer dens belonging to females have the same feature —a nesting chamber located two or three feet below the surface. If a female has an exceptionally large litter, she may dig as many as four nesting chambers to accommodate her babies. All of the chambers are constructed so that they are slightly higher than the floor of the shaft leading to them. This protects them from flooding.

It is easy to distinguish a chuck's den from the dens of other animals. There is always a mound of dirt at its entrance. The mound—which is constantly being made taller as the den's owner brings dirt to the surface—serves as a watchtower and a sun porch. Chucks bury the feces they remove from their toilets under these mounds.

While most winter dens have at least two entrances, dens have been found with a dozen. The main entrance always has a wide opening. This not only permits a chuck to stick its head out and determine whether or not it is safe to emerge but also

Note the platform or lookout station around entrance to burrow. Usually, these steps are occupied by older chucks that have been much hunted.

makes it easier for *monax* to dash underground when being chased. Few predators are able to follow a frightened chuck into its den. About a foot from the entrance, the burrow narrows to five inches or less in width. Moreover, the shaft leading from the opening may make an abrupt turn and then suddenly slope downward.

While chucks make no attempt to hide the location of the main entrance to their summer dens, they take great pains to conceal the openings they use for spy holes and emergency exits. These openings, hidden by vegetation, rocks, or roots, have no telltale mound of dirt in front of them. Reached by side tunnels that branch off the main corridor, the openings are dug from within. As a result, there is little, if any, soil on the surface.

Furred Bulldozers

As indicated, when excavating dens, woodchucks loosen soil with their powerful front feet and kick it backward with the

58

Surprised while enlarging its burrow, this chuck fearlessly faces the photographer. Note the size of some of the stones the "furred bulldozer" has removed.

hindfeet. As soon as they accumulate a load, they shove it out of the burrow with their heads.

The rapidity and efficiency with which woodchucks dig has long astonished zoologists. For example, William Hamilton, an authority on the animals of the eastern United States, writes: "The speed at which excavating is done is amazing. A woodchuck can bury itself from view in a minute, providing the soil is reasonably light and porous. Simple burrows with a single entrance, totaling five feet in length, are completed in a day."

When setting up housekeeping, chucks avoid den sites near occupied burrows. But *monax*, although a solitary animal, will tolerate neighbors if an area is sure to provide plenty of food and protection from enemies. Thus, in certain regions, the local chuck population may average eight animals to an acre. Meanwhile, where farms have been abandoned and fields are slowly being covered by scrub trees and bushes, naturalists consider two chucks to an acre "a dense population."

John Burroughs would have been shocked at these figures. In 1917, while vacationing at his summer home, Woodchuck Lodge in the Catskill Mountains of New York, the famous nature writer estimated that the local woodchuck population totaled 2500 to the square mile!

Woodchuck numbers may have declined but one thing is certain. When autumn's golden days give way to the cold of winter, woodchucks will do what they have always done. Entering their burrows, they will slowly walk along the tunnel to their sleeping chambers. After sealing them tight, they will roll into a ball and, in time, fall asleep. When they awaken from hibernation, it will be spring and time for mating.

5
Man vs. Chuck

"Relationship leads to ill-feeling."
—Latin Proverb

Woodchucks would never win a popularity contest. Because they have ravenous appetites, prefer cultivated crops to wild plants, trample down alfalfa and clover, and are constantly digging, farmers despise them. Indeed, *monax* has been labeled a curse to agriculture that "eats to give himself the strength to dig holes and digs holes to give himself an appetite for more clover."

Most backyard gardeners who have unwillingly provided chucks with vegetarian banquets would be hard pressed to find something complimentary to say about their uninvited guests. Yet Henry David Thoreau, the famous American philosopher, displayed great tolerance toward the woodchucks that raided his garden. In his *Journal* for July 7, 1846, Thoreau notes, "My enemies are worms, cool days, and most of all woodchucks. The last have nibbled for me a quarter of an acre clean. But what right had I to oust johnswort and the rest, and break up their ancient herb garden?"

Thoreau's willingness to share his crops with woodchucks is most unusual. As a matter of fact, chuck-proofing gardens is a major activity wherever chucks are found. In order to keep their plantings safe from marauding woodchucks, gardeners resort to various devices. Some individuals scatter mothballs along the perimeters of their gardens in hopes that the odor will repel "the ingenious vegetarians." Others enclose their plots with electric fences. Still others take more direct action—they shoot chucks on sight, train dogs to kill the "varmints," or drop bombs containing a lethal gas down burrow entrances.

There are those who are convinced that if chucks, visiting a garden for the first time, happen to take a bite out of the leaf of an eggplant, pepper, squash, or tomato, they will leave immediately and never return. Believers in this bit of gardening lore plant eggplants, peppers, squash, and tomatoes so that they form a "living fence" around other crops. Actually, it is a better practice to "fence" gardens with marigolds, which are bitter-tasting. Marigolds—like the vegetables listed above—may not drive woodchucks away but they do make gardens more pleasing to the eye.

Blooming marigolds have far more eye appeal than a chicken-wire fence of one-inch mesh standing two feet high and buried one foot in the ground. While such a fence supported by stout stakes *may* force chucks to seek "free lunches" elsewhere, there is no guarantee. After all, some groundhogs learn to slip unharmed through electric fences. Thus there is little doubt that a really hungry chuck will find a way to get over or under a chicken-wire barrier, although some chucks make no attempt to bypass mesh fences covered with black polyethylene sheeting. No one knows why this is so—but it well may be that sheeting makes it impossible for the animals to see or to smell the protected vegetation.

Many field naturalists are convinced that woodchucks are blamed for far more crop damage than they actually cause. However, these experts admit that the chuck's skill as an engineer makes it a nuisance to farmers. This is nothing new. In 1883, the Woodchuck Committee of the New Hampshire Legislature, in recommending a ten-cent bounty be placed on the woodchuck, noted that it ". . . burrows beneath the soil, and then chuckles to see a mowing machine, man and all, slump into one of the holes, and disappear." This charge, along with stories of children tumbling down chucks' burrows, are gross exaggerations. So are the majority of tall tales detailing how woodchucks undermined farm buildings.

On the other hand, it is true that the stones and mounds of dirt at den openings, when concealed by tall grass, do cause accidents to tractors and also dull the knives and blades of agricultural machinery. But most of the reports of workhorses

Vegetables in kitchen gardens are invitations to hungry chucks. Enclosing plots with electric or wire fences won't always keep a hungry chuck from inviting himself to dinner. Some farmers claim that a perimeter of bitter-tasting marigolds may drive woodchucks away.

Concealed den openings in fields can cause accidents.

injuring their legs by stepping into woodchuck holes are without merit.

In their famous report, the New Hampshire Woodchuck Committee poked fun at the chuck's appearance: "Its body is thick and squatty, and its legs are so short that its belly seems almost to touch the ground. This is not a pleasing picture." But the committee was not content to ridicule the chuck's physical characteristics by calling attention to its "deformities of mind and body." After stating that the woodchuck was a "thief" and a "wayward sinner," the committee declared that it was "absolutely devoid of any interesting qualities."

New Hampshire legislators were not the only politicians to publicly declare their contempt for the woodchuck. A group in Pennsylvania announced that "it had looked in vain for some one redeeming trait in this sneaking curse to the agriculture of our state."

This is most unfair. Despite the fact that woodchucks are a nuisance to farmers and backyard gardeners alike, they play a most important role in the natural order and, in the process, befriend man. For example, many red fox vixens raise their young on woodchuck flesh. When mature, the foxes feed upon field mice and crop-destroying insects such as beetles and grasshoppers, thereby aiding the farmer.

No rodents are more disliked by farmers than field mice, which feed on cultivated crops in both the Old and New Worlds. Because chucks help to keep fox kits alive by providing them with meat, and foxes feed heavily on mice, the woodchuck plays a part in the natural order.

Besides preying on the chucks, red foxes, as indicated, often take up residence in their abandoned dens. The skunk—another insect-eating ally of the farmer—also sets up housekeeping in old chuck burrows. Accomplished diggers, skunks usually enlarge the dens they sublease.

Not only does *monax* help farmers control vermin and harmful insects by furnishing homes to red foxes and skunks but also it renders a valuable service to trappers. Their snares would not capture so many victims if chucks did not provide valuable furbearers with shelter and a place to raise their young. This is not only true of foxes and skunks but also of the mink, muskrats, and otters that frequently take over old woodchuck dens near bodies of water.

Weasels and chipmunks often sneak into the burrows of hibernating woodchucks and make small pockets in the side of the tunnel in which to pass the winter. These "squatters" usually escape eviction unless the owner of the den awakes from his deep sleep exceptionally early.

Domestic cats that have been cruelly abandoned by their owners at the end of a summer vacation also find shelter in abandoned chuck holes. Some burrows are constantly occupied —as fast as one tenant moves out, another moves in, altering the tunnel and chambers to meet its needs. Schoonmaker reports that, "In a den I observed near Rensselaer, New York, I recorded the original owner, the woodchuck; during the winter when the chuck was hibernating, a cottontail rabbit made the den an emergency home. Later, a skunk took possession. Some time after the skunk left, a raccoon moved in, and finally the burrow was used as a nursery for a family of red foxes."

Hunters as well as trappers are indebted to the woodchuck. Unlike domestic rabbits or the wild rabbits of Europe, the

*This young hunter cries
crocodile tears for the fat
chuck he shot.*

cottontail rabbit—the number one small game animal in the
United States—does not dig a burrow. During warm weather,
cottontails sleep in "forms" (depressions made by their bodies
in tall grass). In the winter they take up residence in abandoned woodchuck dens. Cottontails also seek temporary sanc-
tuary in burrows when chased by predators. Thus, according to
the noted wildlife photographer/writer Leonard Lee Rue, III,
". . . rabbits would be far more limited in the eastern states if
they had no woodchuck burrows to use for homes and for escape from their enemies."

When most gardeners shoot a chuck that has been raiding
their vegetables, they bury the carcass. But there are those who
hunt woodchucks for meat. Because *monax* only feeds on green
vegetation, its flesh is delicious. However, care must be taken
to remove the three glands filled with the yellowish-white fluid
that gives chucks their characteristic odor. Incidentally, most

individuals who shoot woodchucks for meat do not go hunting until midsummer. As a result, there is little danger of their killing females with babies too young to care for themselves.

It would be extremely difficult to convince most farmers that woodchucks improve their fields and pastures. Nevertheless, they do. When chucks dig their dens they bring subsoil to the surface, where it is exposed to the weather. Eventually, this dirt breaks up and forms topsoil. Meanwhile, the long tunnels connecting the various chambers in dens allow air to penetrate underground. This also aids in breaking up subsoil. In addition, whenever water seeps into abandoned burrows, it mixes organic material with the soil.

The subsoil carried to the surface each year by woodchucks would make a huge mountain. Hamilton estimates that, in New York State alone, chucks bring some 1,600,000 tons of earth to the surface yearly. This is the equivalent of 52,000 carloads of dirt, each weighing fifty tons!

Some thirty years ago scientists began observing hibernating woodchucks in hopes of finding out how they withstood extremely cold temperatures. This investigation led to research into the possibility of inducing hibernation in humans. If this could be done, the need of space explorers for food and oxygen would be greatly reduced and, theoretically, astronauts could travel for light-years without aging.

Today, in university laboratories throughout the United States, biochemists, psychologists, and medical technicians are still attempting to solve the puzzle of hibernation. If they can discover how a woodchuck's brain senses temperature changes and sends messages to the body to speed up or to slow down its activities, we will have "a clearer understanding of the human brain and the mystery of sleep."

68

Woodchucks choose protected nesting sites where rocks make it difficult for a predator to enlarge the tunnel. It is estimated that in New York State alone, these furred bulldozers bring over a million and a half tons of subsoil to the surface yearly, thus enriching the soil.

Moreover, if an investigation reveals how and why chucks sleep soundly through the cold of winter we may be able to perform routinely, by lowering a patient's temperature during an operation, surgical procedures presently thought too dangerous. Then, too, successful techniques for the treatment of cancer may be developed—many malignancies do not grow in hibernating animals.

Pity the poor woodchuck!

Its helpfulness to man and its aid to wildlife is ignored. But the chuck's raids on gardens are never forgotten. Perhaps *monax* will be considered a pest until research into the ways of the woodchuck leads to the synthesis of a hibernating drug that will greatly benefit mankind. But such a drug may not be perfected for decades.

Meanwhile, hundreds of chucks are killed yearly by trap, poison, and gas. Indeed, there are those who would be delighted if chucks became extinct. Think what a loss it would be if future generations were unable to see "the monarch of the meadow" squatting at the entrance to a den. This must not happen! Nor will it, if we are wise enough to accept Thoreau's conviction that the woodchuck has as much right to live as do the humans who share its world.

Index